821

821.008036

SEA

Selected by
Robert Hull

Illustrated by
Annabel Spenceley

Thematic Poetry

Animal Poetry
Christmas Poetry
Green Poetry
Sea Poetry

Series editor: Catherine Ellis
Designer: Derek Lee

First published in 1991 by
Wayland (Publishers) Ltd
61 Western Road, Hove
East Sussex BN3 1JD, England

© Copyright 1991 Wayland
(Publishers) Ltd

**British Library Cataloguing in
Publication Data**
Sea poetry. – (Thematic poetry)
    I. Hull, Robert   II. Series
    821

    ISBN 0 7502 0172 X

Picture acknowledgements
The publishers would like to thank the
following for allowing their illustrations
to be reproduced in this book: Bruce
Coleman front cover, 5, 7, 8, 13, 15, 27,
28, 31, 32, 35, 40, 43; Greenpeace back
cover, 23, 38, 45; Frank Lane Picture
Agency 19 (© Silvestris); Topham 11, 16;
ZEFA 24.

Typeset by Kalligraphic Design Ltd,
Horley
Printed in Italy by G. Canale &
C.S.p.A., Turin
Bound in France by A.G.M.

Acknowledgements
For permission to reprint copyright ma-
terial the publishers gratefully acknow-
ledge the following: Hamish Hamilton
Ltd for 'Song of the Sea and People' from
When I Dance by James Berry © 1988
James Berry; Rebecca Gaskell for 'Last
Mile of a Holiday'; Irene Rawnsley for 'A
Trip to the Seaside': The James Reeves
Estate for 'Grim and Gloomy' © James
Reeves from *The Wandering Moon and
Other Poems* (Puffin Books) by James
Reeves; 'Until I Saw the Sea' from *I Feel
the Same Way* by Lilian Moore, © 1967
by Lilian Moore. Reprinted by permis-
sion of Marian Reiner for the author; 'The
Sea' © R. S. Thomas, 53 Gloucester Road,
Kew, UK; 'Beachcomber' reprinted by
permission of John Murray (Publishers)
Ltd from *Selected Poems 1954-1983*.
"Fishermen with Ploughs" © George
Mackay Brown 1971; 'Fish Pie with Or-
chestra' reprinted by permission of Faber
and Faber from *Dragonsfire and Other
Poems* by Judith Nicholls; 'Page One'
reprinted by permission of Methuen
Children's Books from *Ask a Silly Ques-
tion* by Irene Rawnsley. While every ef-
fort has been made to secure permission,
in some cases it has proved impossible
to trace the copyright holders. The pub-
lishers apologise for this apparent negli-
gence.

Contents

Introduction

'Oh I do like to be beside the seaside' is how the old song goes. And we do. We like to swim, build sandcastles, take donkey rides, buy ice-creams. We skim stones, go beachcombing, look for crabs in rock pools. We stand and watch the sea in its angry winter moods, when great waves thump against the sea-wall. We like just listening to it, especially on a quiet night when it whispers to us.

Then there are all the things you can do on the sea and in it. You can sail, surfboard, water-ski, fall in . . . You can even – if you've got barrels of money – go on cruises round the world, or cross the Atlantic to do Christmas shopping.

Some people spend their working lives on the sea. Then it's not just for fun anymore. It's dangerous, sailing out into winter mist and wind to catch fish, living for weeks on oil-mining platforms, diving for pearls. 'The old grey Widow-maker', is what one poet calls the sea.

There seems to be no end to the things we do in, or on, or beside the sea, just as there's no end to the sea itself, and no end of poems written about the sea.

You could think of your own mind as a small sea. Listen to it, see what you can find washed up at the edge of it. Peer in its rock pools. What is that glinting there in the dark, on the sandy bottom?

Until I Saw the Sea

Until I saw the sea
I did not know
that wind
could wrinkle water so.

I never knew
that sun
could splinter a whole sea of blue.

Nor
did I know before
a sea breathes in and out
upon a shore.

LILIAN MOORE

Harp Song of the Dane Women

What is a woman that you forsake her,
And the hearth-fire and the home-acre,
To go with the old grey Widow-maker?

She has no house to lay a guest in –
But one chill bed for all to rest in,
That the pale suns and the stray bergs nest in.

She has no strong white arms to fold you,
But the ten-times-fingering weed to hold you –
Out on the rocks where the tide has rolled you.

Yet, when the signs of summer thicken,
And the ice breaks, and the birch-buds quicken,
Yearly you turn from our side, and sicken –

Sicken again for the shouts and the slaughters.
You steal away to the lapping waters,
And look at your ship in her winter-quarters.

You forget our mirth, and talk at the tables,
The kine in the shed and the horse in the stables –
To pitch her sides and go over her cables.

Then you drive out where the storm-clouds swallow,
And the sound of your oar-blades, falling hollow,
Is all we have left through the months to follow.

Ah, what is Woman that you forsake her,
And the hearth-fire and the home-acre,
To go with the old grey Widow-maker?

RUDYARD KIPLING

Song of the Sea and People

Shell of the conch was sounded,
sounded like foghorn.
Women rushed to doorways,
to fences, to gateways, and watched.
Canoe made from cotton tree
came sailing shoulder high, from up
mountain-pass down to the sea.
They stared
at many men under canoe.
The mothers and children stared.

Shell of the conch was sounded,
sounded like foghorn.
Women rushed to seaside.
Canoes had come in,
come in from way out
of big sea, loaded
with fish, crabs and lobsters.
They stared
at sea-catch.
The mothers and children stared.

Shell of the conch was sounded,
sounded like foghorn.
Women rushed to seaside.
Canoe out of cotton tree had thrown men,
thrown them into deep sea.
Deep sea swallowed men.
Big sea got boat back.
They stared
at empty canoe.
The mothers and children stared.

JAMES BERRY

Morning Conversation

'Hi!' said Adur II to Christie Sue.
'Bye!' said Fire Fly to Lady Di.
'Going out?' said Yerba Buena to Little Meranda.
'Coming in?' said Tracy Lee to Pilot 3
and Elias JR.
Anastasia
Petronella
Laguana
Jenny Wren
Arco Thames
Leo
and Shafino
were all having a morning chat in the harbour.

PAUL BURNS (Aged 11)

13

A Trip to the Seaside

Toughen up, kids!
the newsman on TV
said there's forty miles
of traffic jam
from here to the sea.

Eat your crisps,
read your comics,
turn the window down for air;
you know you'll all enjoy it
as soon as we get there.

So you're feeling like
a tin of beans,
cooked and canned?
Think of arcades of amusements,
sea breezes, golden sand.

Count your money,
watch the scenery,
tell jokes and play 'I spy'.
Don't bash the baby's bucket;
it'll only make him cry.

We've made it!
Here's a parking space,
fish and chips to eat!
a walk along the promenade,
the ocean at our feet!

You kids can go exploring
but don't go too far.
In an hour and a half
we want you back,
INSIDE THE CAR!

IRENE RAWNSLEY

Wish You Were Here

Midbay-on-Sea, August 9

Dear Kevin,
        Thought I'd drop a line
with kind regards to everyone.
Wish you were here to share the fun.
Arrived in rain last Saturday,
And will it stop? No blooming way –
Looks like going on for weeks.
Our caravan has fifteen leaks:
It's saturated all our gear.
Kevin, love, wish you were here.
Dad wishes that he hadn't come,
Yesterday he hurt his thumb:
Trapped it in a folding chair –
You should have heard him curse and swear!
He says the beer down here's no good.
The beach has got no sand – just mud;
And what's between us and the sea?
You'll never guess – a cemetery;
When I'm out walking with the pup
I go that way – it cheers me up.
My new swimsuit gave Mum a fit:
She says there's not enough of it.

Closing now, Kev, I'm off to bed,
Think I've got flu, I feel half-dead.
Hoping from this exciting whirl,
You're not out with some other girl.
Much love from Misery-on-Sea,
Wish you were here,
        Your girl-friend,
          G.

ERIC FINNEY

17

Diving for Sunken Treasure

If I could swim like one I know
(Perhaps I shouldn't tell his name)
And dive as deeply as he dives,
I'd very gladly do the same . . .
It would be fine to walk in flippers
Instead of sandals, shoes or slippers.

I'd like to put a wet-suit on,
A helmet with a window, too,
And tumble backwards from a boat
Into a world all strange and new –
A water-world of wild commotion
Swirling about me in the ocean.

The rolling waters overhead,
The endless movements all about,
The fishes never known before,
The seaweed weaving in and out,
But most of all, the greatest pleasure
Would be in seeking sunken treasure.

For wrecks beneath the ocean lie
Filled full of riches, so they say;
Cargoes of precious stones and gold
Gathered from countries far away,
Buried such fearful fathoms under . . .
Could it be ever found, I wonder?

ELIZABETH FLEMING

The Eddystone Light

Me father was the keeper of the Eddystone Light,
He married a mer-my-aid one night;
Out of the match came children three –
Two was fish and the other was me.

When I was but a boyish chip,
They put me in charge of the old lightship;
I trimmed the lamps and I filled 'em with oil,
And I played Seven-up accordin' to Hoyle.

One evenin' as I was a-trimmin' the glim
An' singin' a verse of the evenin' hymn,
I see by the light of me binnacle lamp
Me kind old father lookin' jolly and damp;
An' a voice from the starboard shouted 'Ahoy!'
An' there was me gran'mother sittin' on a buoy –
Meanin' a buoy for ships what sail
An' not a boy what's a juvenile male.

Jolly stories, jolly told
When the winds is bleak and the nights is cold;
No such life can be led on the shore
As is had on the rocks by the ocean's roar.

ANON

Seven-up: *a card game*

A Dream of Drowning

Methought I saw a thousand fearful wrecks;
A thousand men that fishes gnaw'd upon;
Wedges of gold, great anchors, heaps of pearl,
Inestimable stones, unvalu'd jewels,
All scatter'd in the bottom of the sea.
Some lay in dead men's skulls; and in these holes
Where eyes did once inhabit, there were crept,
As 'twere in scorn of eyes, reflecting gems,
That woo'd the slimy bottom of the deep,
And mock'd the dead bones that lay scatter'd by.

WILLIAM SHAKESPEARE
Richard III, (I, iv)

I Started Early – Took My Dog

I started Early – Took my Dog –
And visited the Sea –
The Mermaids in the Basement
Came out to look at me –

And Frigates – in the Upper Floor
Extended Hempen Hands –
Presuming Me to be a Mouse –
Aground – upon the Sands –

But no Man moved Me – till the Tide
Went past my simple Shoe –
And past my Apron – and my Belt
And past my Bodice – too –

And made as He would eat me up –
As wholly as a Dew
Upon a Dandelion's Sleeve –
And then – I started – too –

And He – He followed – close behind –
I felt His Silver Heel
Upon my Ankle – then my Shoes
Would overflow with Pearl –

Until We met the Solid Town –
No One He seemed to know
And bowing with a Mighty look –
At me – The Sea withdrew –

EMILY DICKINSON

Beachcomber

Monday I found a boot –
Rust and salt leather.
I gave it back to the sea, to dance in.

Tuesday a spar of timber worth thirty bob.
Next winter
It will be a chair, a coffin, a bed.

Wednesday a half can of Swedish spirits.
I tilted my head.
The shore was cold with mermaids and angels.

Thursday I got nothing, seaweed,
A whale bone,
Wet feet and a loud cough.

Friday I held a seaman's skull,
Sand spilling from it
The way time is told on kirkyard stones.

Saturday a barrel of sodden oranges.
A Spanish ship
Was wrecked last month at The Kame.

Sunday, for fear of the elders,
I sit on my bum.
What's heaven? A sea chest with a thousand gold coins.

GEORGE MACKAY BROWN

Grim and Gloomy

Oh, grim and gloomy,
So grim and gloomy
Are the caves beneath the sea.
Oh, rare but roomy
And bare and boomy,
Those salt sea caverns be.

Oh, slim and slimy
Or grey and grimy
Are the animals of the sea.
Salt and oozy
And safe and snoozy
The caves where those animals be.

Hark to the shuffling,
Huge and snuffling,
Ravenous, cavernous, great
   sea-beasts!
But fair and fabulous,
Tintinnabulous,
Gay and fabulous are
   their feasts.

Ah, but the queen of the sea,
The querulous, perilous sea!
How the curls of her tresses
The pearls on her dresses,
Sway and swirl in the waves,
How cosy and dozy,
How sweet ring-a-rosy
Her bower in the deep-sea caves!

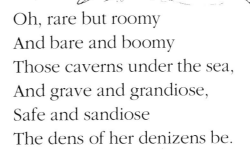

Oh, rare but roomy
And bare and boomy
Those caverns under the sea,
And grave and grandiose,
Safe and sandiose
The dens of her denizens be.

JAMES REEVES

Once the Wind

Once the wind
said to the sea
I am sad

    And the sea said
Why

    And the wind said
Because I
am not blue like the sky
or like you

    So the sea said what's
so sad about that

      Lots
of things are blue
or red or other colours too
    but nothing
neither sea nor sky
can blow so strong
or sing so long as you

    And the sea looked sad
    So the wind said
Why

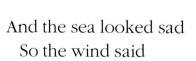

SHAKE KEANE

30

The Sea

They wash their hands in it.
The salt turns to soap
In their hands. Wearing it
At their wrists, they make bracelets
Of it; it runs in beads
On their jackets. A child's
Plaything? It has hard whips
That it cracks, and knuckles
To pummel you. It scrubs
And scours; it chews rocks
To sand; its embraces
Leave you without breath. Mostly
It is a stomach, where bones,
Wrecks, continents are digested.

R. S. THOMAS

Sea-Weed

Sea-weed sways and sways and swirls
as if swaying were its form of stillness;
and if it flushes against fierce rock
it slips over it as shadows do, without hurting itself.

D. H. LAWRENCE

Evening

How long the day:
The boat is talking
with the shore.

SHIKI

The Ocean

The springtime sea:
all day long up and down,
up and down gently.

BUSON

35

The Ballad of the Oysterman

It was a tall young oysterman lived by the river-side,
His shop was just upon the bank, his boat was on the tide;
The daughter of a fisherman, that was so straight and slim,
Lived over on the other bank, right opposite to him.

It was the pensive oysterman that saw a lovely maid,
Upon a moonlight evening, a-sitting in the shade!
He saw her wave her handkerchief, as much as if to say,
'I'm wide awake, young oysterman, and all the folks away.'

Then up arose the oysterman, and to himself said he,
'I guess I'll leave the skiff at home, for fear that folks should
    see;
I read it in the story-book, that, for to kiss his dear,
Leander swam the Hellespont – and I will swim this here.'

And he has leaped into the waves, and crossed the shining
    stream,
And he has clambered up the bank, all in the moonlight
    gleam;
Oh, there were kisses sweet as dew, and words as soft as rain,
But they have heard her father's step, and in he leaps again!

Out spoke the ancient fisherman: 'Oh, what was that, my
    daughter?'
''Twas nothing but a pebble, sir, I threw into the water.'
'And what is that, pray tell me, love, that paddles off so fast?'
'It's nothing but a porpoise, sir, that's been a-swimming past.'

Out spoke the ancient fisherman: 'Now bring me my harpoon!
I'll get into my fishing-boat, and fix the fellow soon.'
Down fell that pretty innocent, as falls a snow-white lamb!
Her hair drooped round her pallid cheeks, like seaweed on a
    clam.

Alas for those two loving ones! she waked not from her
    swound,
And he was taken with the cramp, and in the waves was
    drowned!
But Fate has metamorphosed them, in pity of their woe,
And now they keep an oyster-shop for mermaids down
    below.

OLIVER WENDELL HOLMES

The Sailor's Consolation

One night came on a hurricane,
　The sea was mountains rolling,
When Barney Buntline turned his quid
　And said to Billy Bowling;
'A strong nor-wester's blowing, Bill;
　Hark, don't ye hear it roar, now?
Lord help 'em, how I pities them
　Unhappy folks on shore now!

'Foolhardy chaps who live in towns,
　What danger they are all in,
And now lie quaking in their beds,
　For fear the roof should fall in;
Poor creatures! how they envies us,
　And wishes, I've a notion,
For our good luck, in such a storm,
　To be upon the ocean!

'And as for them who're out all day
　On business from their houses,
And late at night are coming home,
　To cheer their babes and spouses,
While you and I, Bill, on the deck
　Are comfortably lying,
My eyes! what tiles and chimney-pots
　About their heads are flying!

'And very often have we heard
　How men are killed and undone
By overturns of carriages,
　By thieves, and fires in London;
We know what risks all landsmen run,
　From noblemen to tailors:
Then, Bill, let us thank Providence
　That you and I are sailors.'

CHARLES DIBDIN

Fish Pie with Orchestra

You can scrabble with a scallop
       or a lobster,
you can tussle with a mussel
       or a crab;
you can whet your appetite
       with whelks or winkles,
or dangle from the pier
       for plaice or dab.
You can hear the noisy
       oyster-catcher fishing,
the ringing of the curlew's
       long 'coo-lee';
the tapping of the turnstone
       seeking supper,
the whispered song sung by
       the rolling sea.

JUDITH NICHOLLS

Page One

Jim and Jane go to the seaside.
It is sunny. They do not fight.
They play with Rags the dog.
He does not bite.

Mummy and Daddy smile.
The toy shop lady smiles.
The man in the café smiles.
Jim and Jane smile.
Rags smiles.
They all smile, in reading books.

IRENE RAWNSLEY

Last Mile of a Holiday

We watched the town
fall back behind the cliff
and felt the boat
start to lift and dip.

We raised binoculars
at passing beaches
and bays where nothing
seemed to be happening.

Two hours slid by
of only islands
and cliffs and flying
fish making quick

twenty-yard dashes
away from us leaving
grooves of dark
on the swaying stillness.

The boat was already
nearing harbour
when we heard the cry –

And there! A dark fin
in a fold of the wake
and a face nosing up spray
like a submarine

from just under the surface
– a kind of grin
where its mouth was –
then a dozen or so more

up ahead, not chasing,
their slow
black fins following
each other over

in a continuous
revolving movement
like the teeth of a huge
saw. It was the still,

blue sun-filled
old sea simply
showing us
why we came.

REBECCA GASKELL

43

Biographies

James Berry lives in Brighton, on the south coast of England. His recent book of poems – *When I Dance* – won the Signal Poetry Award, for poems written for children. He uses Caribbean rhythms and language in many of his poems, but he says that he wants us to read them in 'our own, natural easy voice'.

George Mackay Brown is one of Scotland's finest poets and short-story writers. He lives where he has always lived, in Stromness, in the Orkney Islands. He has written a lovely book about the Orkneys, called *An Orkney Tapestry*.

Paul Burns was 11 when he wrote the poem we have included here. We don't know where he is now, but he should be about 18, if our arithmetic is right.

Charles Dibdin (1745–1814) was born in Southampton, England. He wrote two novels, many plays and over a thousand songs, many about the sea. 'Tom Bowling', 'Poor Jack' and 'Blow High, Blow Low' are some of the best known.

Emily Dickinson (1830–86) was one of the greatest American poets. She was very unlucky, because publishers and friends thought her poems were 'strange' and no one was willing to publish a book of them until after she died. Even then, publishers often changed her punctuation, and even altered some of the words she had written. She could say a great deal in a few short lines.

Eric Finney has written two books of poems for children. The most recent one is called *Billy and Me at the Church Hall Sale*.

Rebecca Gaskell was born in 1935 in the north of England. She writes poetry for children and adults.

Oliver Wendell Holmes (1809–94) was professor of anatomy and physiology at Harvard University, but he also wrote stories and poems. Some of his poems are very amusing.

Shake Keane was born in St Vincent, in the West Indies, in 1927. He has published a book of poems called *The Volcano Suite.*

Rudyard Kipling was born in Bombay in 1865. He worked as a journalist and wrote his first poems and stories for newspapers and for the Indian Railway Library. He wrote lots of stories for children. After leaving India, he lived in Vermont for a while, and then in England, in Sussex, where he died in 1936. He was the first English writer to receive the Nobel Prize.

D. H. Lawrence (1885–1930) was a famous novelist who also wrote many poems. Some of his best-loved poems are about creatures and flowers.

Judith Nicholls has written several books of poems for children, and she broadcasts regularly on radio and television. She often holds writing workshops with children in schools.

Irene Rawnsley lives in Settle, Yorkshire. In 1988 Methuen published a collection of her poems for children called *Ask a Silly Question*, and a second book, called *Dog's Dinner,* was published in 1990.

James Reeves (1909–1978) was born near London. He wrote over thirty books, many of them books of poems for children.

William Shakespeare (1564–1616) was born in Stratford-on-Avon. He moved from there to London, to make a name for himself in the theatre. He wrote many great plays and poems, which have become very famous. They have been translated into many different languages, and are performed today all over the world.

R. S. Thomas was born in Cardiff in 1913. He became a priest in 1937. He really wrote for adults, but younger people also enjoy many of his moving, straightforward poems about people he met through his work as a priest. He was awarded the Queen's Medal for Poetry in 1964.

Index of first lines